EPIPHANIES & ELEGIES
VERY SHORT STORIES

BRIAN DOYLE

A SHEED & WARD BOOK

ROWMAN & LITTLEFIELD PUBLISHERS, INC.
Lanham • Boulder • New York • Toronto • Plymouth, UK

A SHEED & WARD BOOK

ROWMAN & LITTLEFIELD PUBLISHERS, INC.

Published in the United States of America
by Rowman & Littlefield Publishers, Inc.
A wholly owned subsidiary of The Rowman & Littlefield Publishing Group, Inc.
4501 Forbes Boulevard, Suite 200, Lanham, Maryland 20706
www.rowmanlittlefield.com

Estover Road
Plymouth PL6 7PY
United Kingdom

British Library Cataloguing in Publication Information Available

Library of Congress Cataloging-in-Publication Data

Doyle, Brian, 1956 Nov. 6-
   Epiphanies & elegies : very short stories / Brian Doyle.
      p. cm.
   "A Sheed & Ward Book."
   Includes bibliographical references and index.
   ISBN-13: 978-1-58051-204-6 (alk. paper)
   ISBN-10: 1-58051-204-6 (alk. paper)
   I. Title.
PS3604.O9547E65 2007
821'.92—dc22   2006023102

Printed in the United States of America

⊚™ The paper used in this publication meets the minimum requirements of
American National Standard for Information Sciences—Permanence of Paper
for Printed Library Materials, ANSI/NISO Z39.48-1992.

to
Pattiann Rogers,
a superb poet & gracious soul

&

to
my clan brother Ben Birnbaum,
a fine poet & holy heart

Other Books by Brian Doyle

(essays)

Two Voices (with Jim Doyle)
Credo
Saints Passionate & Peculiar
Leaping
Spirited Men

(nonfiction)

The Wet Engine
The Grail

Poems, essays, stories,
they are all fictions . . .
Our fictions are attempts
to bring the world
into order for the time being . . .

—ALASTAIR REID

CONTENTS

I. POEMS IN PRAISE OF
WILD HOLY ANIMALS

II. POEMS IN PRAISE OF WILD HOLY CHILDREN

III. Poems of War

IV. Poems in Irish

V. PRAYER POEMS

VI. Elegies & Eulogies

I

POEMS IN PRAISE
OF WILD HOLY
ANIMALS

To the Sparrow
Inside the Terminal
Near Gate B25
at the Denver Airport

Hey, little dude, good luck with that spring roll
Twice your size. And beware the scary red sauce,
Which is from a galaxy far far away. And avoid
The guy shouting into his shirt collar, and the kid

With the tennis racket hunting for you, and why
His mother let him extract the racket from her bag
Is a total mystery to me, and beware the snaking cart
Careening past filled with tiny silent nuns, & avoid

The gate agent who is exhausted and besieged, and
Beware me too, little brother, even me, who attends
To your verve and energy and guzzling of red sauce,
For so very often what we notice we then destroy.

So let's pretend we didn't see each other at all a bit,
And neither of us wondered if that awful sticky red
Gluck is actually melted plastic or what, and I didn't
Eventually go home and write this poem. What poem?

DEATH OF A PHOEBE

Slain on the lawn
Near dawn.
Cause of death,
Severed spinal cord,
Leading to loss of brain function
And cessation of mobility in the body
Which is a stiffening shock in the grass.

The cat paces, waiting for the wake to end.
My sons pray: God, make the bird better.
My daughter prays: God, kill the cat.

I pray: God, let me die before they do,
Let me not see them broken and pale upon cold tables and beds,
Let me not see them weeping with evil fires in the cores of their
     bodies,
Let me not see them badly married, lonely, lost in the webs of their
     minds,
Let them weep for me silent with my feathers unruffled & wearing
     my good shoes,
About to be borne to a hole in the grass & returned unto the dust
     from which I came.

HOLDING A SWIFT

Its huge black feet
As thin and black as wires,
Its raving black eye clapped on me like a coat.

It shot out of the fireplace smoke
Like a soft knife and hooked
Itself on the doorjamb and when

I reach for it with a towel it slumps
Into my hands like a small child
Surrendering finally to sleep.

It weighs nothing,
It is as soft as dusk,
Its heart thunders.

On the porch I open my hands
And it is a sudden dark slice in the air
A bright line remembering where it used to be.

MINKING THE BOOTS

While my daughter is outside
Wearing her old boots one more time,
I am minking and thinking of the mink who thought
About his or her daughters and sons too, no question,
In some minkish way that I do not yet know but maybe
Can feel if I mink the boots carefully with what remains
Of the mink. Odd to be diligently working oil from the skin
Of a mink into the skin of a cow, so that the boots will be soft
On the supple skin of my daughter, but such is the nature of love,
The working and working of skins one on another in pursuit of grace.

DEBEEING THE BEE

I watch as a jay grabs and begins violently
And carefully to edit a large orange bee,
Which struggles valiantly for a moment,
Forcing the jay to hotfoot around for a bit,
But then the bee ceases to be and the jay sets to work
Extracting the beedom of the bee from a small hole in the stern.
The jay with great care and thoroughness deletes the bee nature
From the former bee, husk of bee, the bee which has been de-beed,
And swoops off. My daughter and I make a foray to examine the
Wreckage. But there is no wreckage; the bee is whole but for a hole
The size of a pinhead where his stinger used to be.
Through this miniscule opening the jay somehow
Managed to deftly withdraw whatever it is that is
Nutritious and desirable in bees to scrub jays,
Leaving a bee-looking un-bee on the cedar post.
I think about this, oddly, for the rest of the day,
And keep going back to look at the shell of bee.
It looks so much like a real bee, a live bee, a bee
With zest and purpose, with a dangerous hunger,
But its bee-stuff, the essence of bee, is now the
Essence of jay. There's a metaphor here somewhere,
But I leave it to its own devices, and tickle my daughter.

GOOSE ARRESTED AT CORNER
OF WINTER & SUMMER

True story.
Read it in the paper,
And then walked down to the station
Past corner of Winter and Summer streets
(Looking for signs of struggle)
To talk to cop about it.
He didn't want to talk about it.
You writer guys, he says. Always looking to make us look silly.
Mike, you arrested a goose, I say.
I didn't *arrest* him, he says. I brought him *in*. For his own protection.
Him?
We checked.
What did he do to warrant a ride in the squad car?
Disrupted traffic.
How?
Wouldn't leave the intersection. Attacked two cars.
Damage?
Scratches to cars. Trauma to goose.
Why was he so upset at the cars?
We think he felt it was his intersection.
The cars were trespassing?
Or maybe it's a mating thing. I don't know.
You going to release him?
We're taking him north tomorrow.
Where?
Can't say. Confidential.
What if he comes back?
Well, if he behaves, he's welcome in town.
How will you know he's back if he behaves?
We took his picture. *We'll* know.

FOUR CROWS WRITTEN
LIKE THE NOTES OF A SONG
ON THE WIRES OF A FENCE

Up at the crack of dawn
Woken by the hack of the boy
Upstairs coughing into his blanket,
I make coffee and stare at the misty
Yard emerging outside the window,
A miracle crawling every morning
From its wet dark bed: the cedars,
The walnuts and hollies and filberts,
The butterfly bushes and wisteria,

And then shyly the squirrel with half
A tail and then the quartet of crows
Sitting on the fence waiting
Every morning for the crusts
From the breakfast of the boy
Coughing upstairs. The crows
Are startled to see me this early.
They ripple nervously along the fence.

I don't move.
They stop moving.
The boy coughs.
The squirrel stops moving.
We are all as still as chapels.
The mist wicks off the cedars.
The crows are ancient and patient.
The moment is moist and holy
And lasts all the way until
I break it and save it by writing it down.

Poems in Praise of Wild Holy Animals

THE SHE-FOX

A man tells me a story one star-strewn summer night.
He and his wife and three children live in the woods.
Near their house there were grey foxes with three kits.
One day when my friend was sitting watching the den
A cougar slid into the scene and time just *stopped*, as
My friend said. The foxes emerged, tense and bristling.
The cougar got too close and the female fox attacked
And was killed. The male backed grimly into the den.
My friend said he could hear the kits mewling faintly.
The cougar tried to root the fox out for a while but quit.

As the cougar left it picked up the she-fox and carried her
Off probably to feed its own kits. There was a silence
For a long while, said my friend, and then the male fox
Emerged alone. He went to the spot where his mate died
And licked it for a while and then he let the kits come out.
They wrestled and chased dragonflies and tumbled around
Like all kids do, you know? said my friend. He told me he
Sat there for a long time in the sunlight, up on a rocky scarp,
Thinking how we always want things to *mean* something
But they don't, they just mean what they are, you know?

→

How Swallows Stitch
the World Together

It's all those loops, of course, unimaginable
Incalculable zillions every day of the year,
The tiny crews swooping off early to work
Whirring & whirling until the swifts arrive

For the late shift and if you listen carefully
You can hear them razzing & chaffing each
Other overhead & the youngsters gunning their
Engines happily for no reason whatsoever at all.

Sometimes I sprawl in the sea of the grass
And watch and wonder and gape and stare
As one zooms past giggling on a dare
So incredibly fast & close I see a riffle

Flare along his wing as he banks and sheers
Back into the hungry ocean of the air.
Today my son waved to me in just that way,
His hand a bird I savored the rest of the day.

CROW CAUGHT IN RUNDOWN
BETWEEN SECOND AND THIRD

Runners on first and third, one out, the boy
At bat the size of a fire hydrant, his huge cap
Pulled grimly over his eyes, and the crow lands
With a plop, and the catcher jumps up *to throw out
The crow!* But he hesitates, not real sure where to go:
Did coach say cut off the run or go for the easiest out?
Because the kid at first looks to be the easiest out, he's
Picking his nose as his dad is barking from the lawn chairs
To *please* pay attention! The crow feints toward third base.
The runner at third, seeing the situation, takes a cautious lead.
The catcher, choosing action, rolls the ball slowly to the pitcher.
The pitcher, shocked, spins to survey the infield and the alert crow
Hops back toward second. The second baseman hustles to the bag
For a possible throw but the pitcher, rattled, throws to first because
The first baseman is the biggest kid on the team. The catcher flips off
His mask with one hand and sprints down the line to back up the
     play
But that leaves home plate open, because the pitcher is headed toward
The lawn chairs to his mom, and the runner at third breaks for the
     plate,
But the crow, instead of advancing to the open base, suddenly
     jumps into
The air and zooms back over second, and the second baseman ducks
     and drops
His mitt in a puddle, and the run scores, but the dad who has been
     dragooned into
Being umpire calls time and waves off the run and calls in a new
     pitcher, and my
Son and I, having once again witnessed events that are new in the
     world, head home.

Epiphanies & Elegies

12

INSTRUCTIONS TO THE NEW PUPPY

Do not *ever* again for *any* reason eat crayons.

Do not eat more mice in one day than you can digest.

Do continue to eat as many ants and moths as you can slurp.

Do not ever again eat anything that even remotely *resembles* a crayon.

Do continue to make that rubbery surf-guitar sound when I rub your belly.

Do continue to face the heat vent with your eyes closed and a smile on your face.

Do continue to slide across the floor and crash into the wall for no discernible reason.

Do continue to wait impatiently for the children to emerge magically from their rooms.

Do not even think any more about the crayons. For*get* the crayons. Move on. Let it go.

Do not continue to bang on the door with your water dish when you want to come in,

Because even though I admire your intelligent manipulation of the tools handy to paw

To issue messages to creatures who I am sure seem a complete and utter puzzle to you,

And even as I like you personally, your mad eyes, our mutual cautious respectfulness,

I grow weary of mud and chewing and nipping and shouting and sudden puddles

Which look to me like remote mysterious islands in the Malay Archipelago.

So if we are to get along, which it looks like we are going to have to do,

I suggest that you get a grip and stop eating things other than food,

And stop nipping the children and causing chaos and hubbub,
And I will continue to rub your belly when I get home,
And do my very best, as a gentleman, to forget
The whole crayon thing, of which
The less said the better.

Romance: a Note

The male snipe afflicted by love flies upside down.
The male willet in similar straits begins to strut.
The male woodcock flutters helplessly as if shot.

A stilt sandpiper hovers frantically over his love
And then emits a sound like a donkey's bray.
The buff-breasted sandpiper overcome by love

Climbs into a hole and opens wide his wings.
The female object of his attentions, it is said,
Pays no attention to the silent male in his hole.

The male avocet, having fallen for his love,
Stands around with other males all talking at once.
The male sanderling, in the throes of romance,

Stands atop his beloved and pokes her with his bill
Until she consents at last to the press of his attentions.
Female ruffs, after males fight, often choose the loser,

And often then also mate with the winner and any
Other males in the area. Male ruffs, like male wrens,
Mount decoys, other males, and alluring tufts of grass.

The ruddy turnstone is sometimes provoked to courtship
By airplanes and motorboats. The curlew, when infatuated,
Tries to mate in flight. The male phalarope, shy and drab,

Absorbs so many blows from the female that he often hides.
However the male, having once mated, becomes promiscuous.
The female phalarope, having been serviced, attacks the male.

Poems in Praise of Wild Holy Animals

The female willet, when she judges the love act complete,
Tosses her partner over her shoulder and departs in haste.
The male oystercatcher becomes so wrought with ardor

During the jungle of romance that he often attacks bushes.
Many females of many species are bored by incubation.
Avocets and stilts, at the height of courtship, go to sleep.

SHREDS & SHARDS

One time I was driving in the desert
& there was a dead elk on the road &
As I slowed down to be respectful
A raven landed and began to eat. Not
Three seconds later a car roared over
The rise from the other direction and
Smashed the raven and zoomed away.
The bird was hit so hard it lost a wing.
I stopped to see if maybe I could help,
But the raven wriggled across the road
And died as soon as it reached the dirt.

I drove away thinking that there must
Be a metaphor there somewhere, but I
Still can't figure it out. What stays with
Me isn't the dead elk or the dead raven,
Or the guy who could not stop for death,
But how the bird was so desperate for dirt.
It wasn't even in one piece anymore, with
Mere seconds left in its dark & joyful life,
But it crawled on shreds & shards of bones
To reach that holy dust. I wondered then &
I ask you now: what did the raven want?

TINY

One time an American pro football player named Tim Rossovich
Was bored during the steaming sterile endless days of training camp
So he rose after dinner to speak to his huge & rustling teammates
And when he opened his mouth out flew a sparrow, singing.

The moment quickly became legend among the Eagles and
    their fans
Partly because Rossovich also ate beer bottles and drove cars
    off piers
And the like, but recently when I met him and asked him about
    that day
His face lit up and he told me this story. *Man*, you wouldn't
    believe how

Cool that bird was, he said. His name was Tiny. He was a field
    sparrow
With the most beautiful song, a sweet whirring trill that gave me
    the shivers.
He fell into my room one morning when he was real young, two
    weeks maybe,
He could hardly fly, you know, and I fed him and we got to be
    friends, he would

Fly in and out of my room as he liked, and he had a white ring
    around his eye
That always made him look startled, you know? He was cool little
    dude. He loved
Grasshoppers, so me and my teammates were out there on the field
    at dusk every
Night catching hoppers for Tiny. The coaches thought we were all
    nuts, but Tiny

Was something other than football, other than money and work and
   worry, you know?
Well, the way the story is now is that I did that because I was loony,
   crazy old Rosso,
But the fact is it was the last night of camp, and in the morning we
   were all headed
Back to regular life, so me and Tiny hatched a plan for the last
   moment, you know?

And what no one ever says about that moment was that while most
   guys were laughing
Fit to bust there were also a lot of guys crying for reasons that are
   not so easy to figure.
I cried too, man. Sounds crazy, but something about Tiny flying
   around the room singing
Was real sweet and sad. A joke now but then it was something else.
   Like so many things.

II

POEMS IN PRAISE
OF WILD HOLY
CHILDREN

HER SIDE

Of the big bed
Is where they end up at night.
Hardly ever my side.
Only when they are sick.
Or if there's no room on her side
Because there are too many children
Already on her side.
I think her side must be warmer.
It's further away,
And they have to detour
All the way around my side,
But they do it,
One after another,
And end up on her side
At least for a while
Until they fall asleep,
And she returns them
To their small beds
From which they migrate
Eventually back to her side.
This goes on for hours.
Sometimes I feel as if the bed
Is a sort of bus station,
Passengers coming and going
All night long, their feet
Padding up and down the hall.
Sometimes one in a fog gets lost,
And ends up asleep in the bathroom,

Or curled in the hallway like a cat,
Or warm against my chest
On my side.
This doesn't happen much,
And it's almost always
A mistake of navigation;
But I accept the lost boat
As a harbor does, arms open.

WIPING PAUL

He's someone else's son
Here for a few hours
Playing with my sons,
And he's three years old,
And he has to go to the bathroom.

I say *Can you wipe yourself?*
And he says, quietly, no;
Can you help me? he says.
So there I am, wiping Paul,
And thinking of all the kids
Who need help being wiped
In houses other than their own,
All the kids whose parents are
Somewhere else than where
Their children need to be wiped,
And all the someone elses
Wiping someone else's kids.

I help Paul with his buttons.
Wash your hands, Paul, I say,
And he does so, quietly,
And then runs off with the guys.
But I sit there on the tub
Thinking of all those
Someone else's kids
Waiting to be wiped.

WHAT TO PACK

When you are going to the hospital
For heart surgery on your infant son
Who will be there for a week
If he is lucky.
I pack for the week.
One pair cotton pajamas with flap.
He will be lucky.
I pack this statement in his bag.
One pair cotton socks.
His bag is black,
His socks are blue.
One blanket, cotton.
My heart is black.
One blanket, wool.
My fingers are bleeding
Because I am eating them.
One bag of diapers.
I am eating myself like a trapped fox.
One bag of wipes.
My fingers are bleeding on his black bag.
One Junior Policeman badge from local police force.
One Zuni bear fetish with two magic pebbles.
He is sleeping as I am packing.
He is snoring like a walrus.
One blanket, cotton.
My wife carries him out to the car in the rain.
I start the car.

JOE IN THE DARK

Thrashing; ill.
He is a wet electric muscle
In the wet velvet dark.
Now Israel loved Joseph above all his sons
Because he had him in his old age:
And he made him a coat of divers colors.
I strip Joe of his sleeper of divers colors,
I strip him of his shirt the color of shocks of corn,
I strip him of his wet white steaming socks,
Because he is burning burning burning,
The sweat pouring from him in creeks,
His limbs flung on the bed like sticks.
An evil wild beast hath devoured Joseph, said Israel:
I will go down to my son into hell, mourning.
I take the burning boy upon me,
I bring him aboard like a moaning boat.
He is a hot rock on my chest, a coal, a dark fire.
But the Lord was with Joseph, and had mercy upon him,
And when it is nearly dawn he begins to cool,
His rivers run dry and he falls asleep,
And his father with him who loved him
Because he had him in his old age.

JUPITER

Michael LeBeau has wet his pants.
He is Jupiter, the fifth planet, with a mass
318 times that of the earth.
He is soaked.
Even his socks are wet.
He is crying tears of great magnitude.
They are falling on the surface
Of the plaster planet like meteorites.
Michael's father,
With a mass five times that of his son,
Sits in the dark,
Front row far right,
Where he can see the commotion,
Where he can see Miss Oullette's panic,
Where he can see the sixteen quivering moons of his son.
Saturn comforts Jupiter in a reedy silver voice.
Saturn is the sixth planet,
95 times the size of Earth,
Half the size of Michael.
Finally Mars sings Jupiter's part
And the show goes on,
Saturn, Uranus, Neptune, Pluto.
Pluto is a first-grader.
That is the end of the play.
Michael and his father drive home,
Where his father helps him out of his costume.
Michael falls asleep shivering on the couch.
His father looks up the moons of Jupiter
And begins to recite them in the dark:

Adrastea, Amalthea, Ananke
He covers the boy with a blanket
Carme, Callisto, Europa,
Ganymede, Himalia, Sinope,
And sags into his chair
Thebe, Metis, Lysithea,
Pasiphae, Leda, Elara, Io,
And stares at the moon
And falls asleep too.

THE SEA OF THE STARS

My son says to me this morning,
What happens when people die?
And don't give me a dad answer.

I know exactly what he means:
No sermon, no lecture, no blather.
He's after the meat of the thing.

You keep moving somehow, Joe,
I say, like an arrow leaving a bow,
Or light leaving the bedroom when

You flick your lamp off at night.
It jumps out the window & heads
For the hills. You can't quench it

Or touch it or bottle it or save it.
It goes where it goes. Light fills one
Shape for a while & then itches to

Travel on. It's sort of insouciant
That way. Insouciant, says my boy,
Does that mean it's happy or what?

And I sit there and stare at this kid,
Who when you think about it came
To us straight from the sea of the stars,

And I say yup, Joe, as far as can tell,
It's way happy. The start of any trip
Is a pain, but then you get all absorbed,

You know? You just keep going. Okay,
He says, but where will *you* go, and can
I go too? Think about it, dad. We'll talk.

THE WAY THAT FATHERS OF THE GIRLS NAMED GOALKEEPER DRIFT CASUALLY DOWN THE SIDELINE TO STAND BEHIND THE GOAL NET

As if drawn there by some migratory urge,
Some irresistible magnetic force
That compels them to sidle
Unobtrusively down the line
And around the corner
To one goalpost or the other
From which tiny campsite
They keep up a steady patter
Of affectionate warning
To their lanky daughters
Who without exception
Jump up to catch the top bar
And swing from it meditatively
As knots of their teammates swirl
In schools around the flashing ball
Far downfield, beyond consciousness.

The daughters swing,
They adjust their jerseys,
They examine the runes of the grass.

The fathers hum,
Shuffle their feet.
Sip their coffee.
Say *watch out now*,
Say *heads up now*.

The wind blows through the cedars
On the south side of the field. A hawk
Lifts off a tree like a brown tent opening.

The ball never comes our way, not once,
But we keep talking the whole second half,
Talking about this and that and the other thing.

Best game of the season.
Best game *ever*.

In Case You Find a Game

In the old days I carried a basketball on my bicycle.
I went nowhere without it just in case I found a game.
We played everywhere, my brothers and I, playgrounds
And parks and streets and gyms and alleys and driveways
Beyond counting. I wore the nubs off any number of balls.

Later I played in other towns and counties and states
And even countries here and there, once deep in Mayo,
The fields around us bright and wet, the basket tired and bent.

Now all these years later there is a ball in the back of my car.
An old ball, worn and perfect. I found it there this morning
And asked my sons what was up and they said *We put it*
There in case of a game, dad. You want to have a ball
Around, you know? Just in case you find a game.

SECRET

My sons are draped on me
In a back pew in church
One on each shoulder
Like warm epaulets.

One is asleep and the other
Is muttering wetly in my ear.

He is telling me a secret,
But I can't make out
A single syllable of the secret.
It's a really *secret* secret.

I say to him later,
What was the secret?
He says he can't tell me:
It's a secret. He says,
I gave it in your ear
And then I had to forget it too.
Those are the rules, he says.

FIRST CONFESSION

Brendan is eleven years old
But hasn't made his confession yet.
He says he's not nervous but he is.

Elizabeth hums and prays.
The Lynch brothers in their
Matching suits sit quietly.

The confessional opens and
Willie emerges and kneels
So close to his mama it's like
He's trying to crawl back in.

Then it's Brendan's turn and
As he slides around the corner
To the booth he looks at me
With those wet black eyes.

Then Lauren. She's deaf,
But she goes in without her mom.

Then her mom asks if she can cut the line
And go in herself, as she hasn't been
In twenty years, and I say sure,
And the kids all stare at Lauren's mom.

Soon it's my son Joe's turn.
I know him well enough not to help.
He buttons his jacket all the way up
And in he goes.

I hear Father's voice rumbling gently.
I don't hear Joe.
I watch a bee by the ceiling.

Soon Joe emerges and walks up the aisle
To say his prayers,
But he pauses where I sit
Confused and moved by the whole thing,
And we stare at each other
For a long minute, his eyes
Stunning.

IN THE PIONEER CEMETERY
NEAR DAMASCUS, OREGON

My wife's father, whom I never met,
And his grandson, whom I never met,
Are buried side by side in the country.

We stop and visit sometimes when we
Are driving by. You climb a tiny hill
And there they are under cedar and fir.

It's a really old cemetery, laid out long
Before the civil war, long before our state
Was a state, and I wander around reading

Sometimes while my wife talks to her dad
& her nephew. Her nephew is not the only
Kid here. There are so very many. I count

Seven who don't even have names. *Infant,*
It says on the stone. *Baby.* In the far corner
There are nameless twin boys near the fence.

So many children. One time I wrote down
Every child under the age of eleven. There
Were twelve of them. Hazel was the oldest.

A tribe, a clan. I imagine Hazel telling Otto
To quit yelling, and Karl and Kent are fighting,
And Hannah and Bertha are down by the creek

Poems in Praise of Wild Holy Children

Looking for crawdads. The little ones nap.
Gustav, who never hardly says a word, goes
To pick berries for everyone. He's a good kid.

Sometimes I get haunted by all the stories
That might have been told about all the kids
Who never grew old. But then you hear a kid

Laughing or yelling at her brothers or maybe
Your twin sons calling to you across the grass
Hey dad! – my favorite two words in the world.

LILIES

My daughter
alp lily
Lily Marie
asparagus
is lean
asphodel
and long
trillium
and lippy
twisted-stalk
and laughing
chive
and rude
chocolate lily
and poignant
common camas
and kind
corn lily
most of the time
death-camas
and I still
fairybells
can't believe
fawn lily
she came to us
fool's onion
ten years ago
garlic
out there

Poems in Praise of Wild Holy Children

glacier lily
she was
great camas
at the table
black lily
this morning
leek
and again
lily-of-the-valley
I reeled
nodding onion
at her sheer lilyness
tiger lily
the prayer she is

Things I Know about Children I Don't Know as Told to Me by My Twin Sons Sprawled like Trout in the Bathtub

Randall loves rocks and is a liar.
Jack can blow bubbles with bubble gum
And can make the bubble go in and out
Of his mouth without popping it.
Ian is the fastest runner.
Kate is the best reader in the class.
Laura is the best writer, though.
She can even write in *cursive*.
Anthony will only play with John.
John steps on people's feet on purpose
And he'll kick you when he's angry.
Joe's brother died last year in his sleep.
Amy's dad died this year. He was a doctor.
Alex wears the same shirt every day.
Zachary is mean to Cole all the time.
Cole is funny but no one plays with him.
Kevin says he smoked a cigarette once
But no one believes him, not even a little bit.
Victoria has really cool sunglasses.
Elizabeth's mom and dad are divorced.
Justin's mom is very fat.
Robert's dad yells at him in front of everybody.
He even yelled at the principal once.
Melissa's sister kisses boys in sixth grade.
Allison is allowed to walk home alone from school.
Corey says he can do things that he can't,
Like ride a bike and do tricks on a skateboard.
Carl wears glasses and loses his temper.
Ariadne likes to draw rabbits.
We don't know *anything* about Molly.

Poems in Praise of Wild Holy Children

NINE

There is a
book asleep
face down on
the chest of
my son who
is sleeping
face up on
me also
face up on
his bed where
we were just
reading when
he hit the
wall after
a long day
being nine
which is he
says cool but
wears you out
by the end
of the day
which is where
we are now
or to be
accurate
he is now
but not me
the dad who
is praying
by watching
his sleeping
holy boy.

POEM FOR MISS LOLA BUTTON,

Age Six, of Melbourne, Australia

Someday, some years from now, not all that many really,
You will remember the moment we stood in the back yard
Of your childhood home in the city, the cheerful chaos
Of it all, the crisp light, the shaggy shed, the thirsty plants,
And you will remember our grinning conversation, the way
You asked me how it could be that we understood each other
Though I spoke American and you spoke Australian, your
Language sunny and hopeful and mine headlong and cocky,
Both languages having escaped the maternal empire at last
To find themselves independent but now scarily responsible
To and for so very many children like you, and I teased you
Gravely, as such was my way then with children, I was shy
Too I suppose, and often hid in the forests of the humorous,
But you would not be distracted by jokes, and pressed me as
To the provenance of the words in our mouths that afternoon,
And I have thought about that ever since, how words are shards
And splinters of long stories, and how my job in this rutted road
Is to gather shattered stories and fit them together, so as to bow
In thanks for a world in which there is such a cool elf as yourself.

POEM FOR MR HARRY BUTTON,

Age Ten, of Melbourne, Australia

Well, you're a guy, so you are already totally ahead in the world
Because you won't have people living inside you who emerge
In wet ways your dad will explain to you right after you read this
    poem.
So that's a plus. Plus our interior plumbing is simpler, all things
    considered,
And to be honest the world is still tilted toward guys in general,
    which is unfair,
But that'll change soon enough, so don't agonize over it. In other
    matters we are
Physically much stronger than women, but this affords us no real
    advantage, as they
Live longer and don't start wars like we do. As regards intellectual
    affairs women are
To be honest a bit quicker and smarter than we are but they are
    liable to think in circles
While we tend to think in straight lines, which can be an advantage,
    except when we stop
Considering or even seeing any other ways and means of thinking,
    which leads back to wars.
This is a problem but we are all working on it, and I would be very
    appreciative if you would
Take a leading role in this matter in the years to come. As regards all
    other questions, see your dad.

AT THE SOCCER FIELD AS THE LAST GAME OF MY DAUGHTER'S SEASON NEARS ITS END

I hear the tides of cheers from the next field,
And turn to watch the end of that game also,
Hood River against Mount Tabor, it ends tied
And goes to a shootout, & the shootout ends up
Tied also, and it goes to sudden death and a girl
From Hood River absolutely *hammers* her shot
Into the remote galaxy of the upper corner and
She sprints ecstatic into a howling sideline sea,

But the Mount Tabor team is sprinting wildly out
Too onto the wet field, racing toward their goal to
Envelop their weeping goalie, they pour from the
Sideline a green and white river of girls with their
Arms stretched toward their friend on her knees,

And the coaches take hesitant steps onto the field,
Not sure if they are welcome in the moment or if
This is a team thing or a girl thing or what, and the
Moms and dads and kid sisters watch quietly too, &
I stand there in the mud between Fields One and Two
Sobbing so hard I have to go hide in the PortaPotty.

BLUE PRAYERS

Walking along the tide line I see a crippled kid
Trailing along behind probably her dad and sisters

And the kid is maybe four years old and her feet are bent
Sideways so the toes face each other, so she sort of hops

Rather than walks, you know? But she's hopping real fast
And laughing and throwing gobs of wet sand at her sisters

And bending suddenly when she sees something cool in the
Wrack and ruin along the line, the shards of crab and whirls

Of kelp and mussel shells open and empty like blue prayers,
And she gets absorbed by a piece of bone or something and

Falls way behind her tribe and her dad calls and she looks up
And laughs and hops amazing fast and when she is a few feet

Away he crouches a little and extends his arm and she shinnies
Right up his arm as graceful and quick as anything you ever saw

And she slides into what must be her usual seat on his neck and off
They go and I mumble *thank you thank you* and then keep going too.

III

POEMS
OF WARS

FAYAD

Here's a tale.
True tale, too.
There's a boy
Nine years old

Walking home
And his arm
Is blown off
By the war

And his arm
Flies into
The old road
And he runs

To get it
And a truck
Nails him good
And he dies.

This could be
Any old war
Any old time,
But it isn't.

SMOKES

for Sergeant Donald Dinsmore,
592nd Engineer Regiment,
U.S. Army Boat Battalion, 1944

One time we went up
On the beach in Leyte
To rescue some guys
Who had been stuck there
For a month under fire
All day every day.

They had broken through
The lines to the sea
And we went to get
As many as we could.

We got twenty-eight guys
Off that little beach
In our two-man boat.
It was a hell of a time.

The waves were monsters
And we snapped a hawser
On our landing gate but we
Figured it somehow and ran
Back to sea fast as we could.

Those guys were zombies.
I asked them if they wanted
Some coffee, we could make it
On a little stove we had, but
They shook their heads no.

I asked them if they wanted
Something to eat, we had cans
Of stuff, but they said no.

They were all in shock,
You know, and couldn't
Hardly speak.

But when I asked them
If they wanted a smoke,
Why, their faces came alive,
And I went around the boat
Lighting smokes and putting
Them in their mouths,

Bending over each guy
And lifting up the brim
Of his helmet to find
His lips.

I came home from the war
To find out smokes killed
My dad, you know,
But if ever there was
A time when they
Weren't coffin nails,
That was the day.

DEATH OF A BYSTANDER

She had gone to get milk
And cookies for the kids'
Lunches the next day.
He thought to take the bus
Instead of walking home
As the day was so fair.
He stopped for a paper.
She popped into the bank.
He paused to read posters
For a band he recalled
From his college days.
She stopped at a fruit stand
For the stunning peaches.
He was identified by his shoes
Which had been resoled twice.
She was identified by her teeth.
A cop found the peaches
And gave them to a child
Who ran all the way home.

THE HONORABLE EDMUND BURKE ADDRESSES MY TWIN SONS AS THEY SULK IN THEIR ROOM AFTER A TERRIFIC FISTFIGHT

We lament these events from experience of their mischief,
Despite sure foresight of their unhappy & inevitable tendency,
And we repeat that we are steadily averse to this civil war
As we are fully persuaded that in such a contest
Victory only varies the mode of your ruin.

Knowing the contemptible value of war,
We have wished to prudently regulate domestic policy,
But disorders have prevailed in the empire;
Not from any misconduct of the government,
But from plans laid in error,
Pursued with obstinacy,
And conducted without wisdom.

You are an exasperated people,
A people in a state of extreme inflammation,
Which seems to us absurd & preposterous
In the face of an austere law.

However hostility may be just or merited,
It is not justifiable or excusable; it is in fact
Human nature effaced by ignorance & barbarity.

All your public declarations which indicate
Anything resembling a disposition to reconciliation,
Seem to us loose, general, equivocal, imprecise,
And unstable, bearing no mark of that native candor
You have formerly exhibited.

We have declared our intention of restoring you to liberty
And are waiting to be informed of what we perfectly know.
We abhor the idea of making a conquest of you
And wish that you would yield to terms of reconciliation;
Thus you shall recover your dominions.

We cannot stand secure upon the principles
Of unconditional submission & passive obedience;
It is in fact from the great principle of liberty itself
That the statutes governing our own rule have originated.

So we confer and treat upon these arduous affairs,
And are sensible of the whole importance of our duty.
We shall with joy & readiness return your attendance
And the alleviation of the complicated evils that oppress us.

Should this not happen, we have discharged our consciences
By this faithful representation & assertion of those principles
Which, in better times, made us a great & admirable empire.

In Absaraka, the Country of the Crows, July 17, 1886

After the skirmish near the Powder River,
A Cheyenne woman ventured out of the brush
Where she had been hiding with her five children.
None of the children were hurt, but the youngest,
A boy of perhaps four years old, naked and torn
By the brambles and thorns of the thicket,
Could not be persuaded to cease his tears.
The woman, now widowed of the teamster Pete,
Said that the attackers had been Oglala,
And that the walk-a-heaps, as she called the troops,
Had pursued the Oglala into the draw, whereupon
The attackers turned, trapped their pursuers,
And cut them to pieces. We gathered the bodies
And returned to the fort. The small Cheyenne boy
Continued his crying all the way in, inconsolable,
Despite the best efforts of the men to cheer him.

THE NEW CREATURES

In the river new creatures squirm
Born of metal eggs & factory sperm,
Carp and turtle, duck and perch
Minnows and rats (river- & musk-),
Grovel in the mud and lurch
Toward the banks to rise at dusk.
Hard cold things never seen before
On the earth, cold fish that tore
Apart old boats and docks and made
The town beach a memory, a shade
Of the warm place it was, and beasts
To make you shiver. No one goes there
Now. At night in the mud there are feasts.

Edward Wood, Lord Halifax, Pauses with Winston Churchill in the Garden at Ten Downing Street, May 9, 1940

> It was a bright, sunny afternoon, and Lord Halifax and I sat
> for a while
> on a seat in the garden, talking about nothing in particular.
> —Churchill, *The Gathering Storm*

The Prime Minister, Chamberlain, having decided to give way
To either Halifax or myself, and our meeting about this matter
Having concluded with the duty in fact fallen upon me,
Which prospect neither excited nor alarmed me,
As I thought it would be by far the best plan,
Halifax and I repaired to the garden.

I remember swallows slipping gaily through the trees
And a brief sense of utter peace that came over us both.
We did not talk of the impending war, or of the way
The leadership of the empire had just been presented
To Halifax, only to be declined by him with a manly grace
Wonderful to behold, but instead we spoke of this and that:

The left hand he had never had, and his three elder brothers
Dead before he was nine years old, leaving him sole heir
To the viscountcy and estates in Yorkshire, and his six years
As viceroy in India, a country he loved and could not forget.
He spoke of the morning light there, how it spilled headlong
Through and over every corner of that land and its people,
Such sweet poor creatures as had ever been born, as he said.

The swallows swam above us and the trees and shrubs burst
Forth with such scent as I rarely remember in all my years.
When after some minutes I found my mind drifting inevitably
To Hitler and Goebbels and Edward's pale meeting with them
Two years previous, and the brooding storm that was soon
To rend the world with bloody rage, I judged it high time
To part with Halifax and return to the Admiralty for heavy business.

He stood to leave also, tall and gaunt, with that long duke's face of his,
His arm held stiffly by his side, and as I reached the gate I saw him
    pause
There under the trees, the swallows wheeling. By that night or
    the next,
I judged, the King would have asked me formally to make a
    government,
And I would at last have the authority to give directions over the
    whole scene.

I thought I knew a good deal about it all and I was sure I should
    not fail,
But there by the gate I did not think of what was to come: I thought
    of Halifax,
And what it must have been like for him as a boy, born to privilege
    but
Without a hand, his brothers dead when he was yet a child,
His manhood only what he could make of it
With the powers of his mind and soul;
A vast load to lay upon a boy.

ANTIPODIAD

John Cadman, age 27, was transported for stealing a horse.
Elizabeth Cadman, age 31, was transported for stealing a knife.
Convicts cut the stones for the prison in which they were held.
In the park are figs and cypress and parrots and ibis in dark pools.
A vast river of fruit bats rushes by the turrets of the cathedral at dusk.
Ironbark and banksia and she-oaks and currawongs and moorhens.
Magpie-larks chortling & burbling & bubbling & humming &
    moaning.
A man tells me that his mother's family refused to attend her
    wedding.
At night I lie in the grass in the park and stare at the wild new stars.
Every morning in the jacaranda tree there is a young crow staring.
A small quick man tells me stories of the time he was a senator.
A big quiet man tells me stories of the red dry hot hard interior.
At noon schoolboys run by me on their way to the rugby field.
The leather handstraps on the tram are so worn that they shine.
A big priest tells me of evictions during the famine in Donegal.
A small priest tells me of his many years on Bougainville Island.
One time, he says, he stood between two armies there all day long.
At the monastery where he lives mynah birds hop through the
    kitchen.
One day in the woods I find a dead possum with bees in its eyes.
One day in a park I find a tree carved with sacred signs and runes.
One day in the city a man tells me a story. It's a bonza story, he says.
Somehow it explains us. When the Dalai Lama came here years ago,
He brought with him four bodhi seeds from the tree of enlightenment
And we planted the seedlings in a peace garden in the heart of
    the city.

The first two seedlings were smashed deliberately by vandals at night.
The third tree was crushed accidentally, we think by exuberant
    lovers,
The fourth tree has been taken to a safe location for its own
    protection.
We may or may not plant it again, depending on where Australia
    goes.

THE FLOGGING OF CHARLES MAHER,
NORFOLK ISLAND, AUSTRALIA, 1823

In the courtyard
On a tripod
Made of pine
That morning
By three men
Who planed the
Logs and fit
An iron cap atop
The meeting-point,
Malone finding the
Metal abandoned
On the scrap heap
By the south wall.

It had been a pot
Carried all the way
From west Kerry
To Sydney Cove,
And o the much use
That old pot had seen!

Now to its last
End it was bent,
And after Maher
Was cut down
In wet ribbons
We were told
To saw the pine
For the fire
Which we did,

But no orders
Being issued
As to the pot,
Malone took it
And flung it
Over the wall
With all his might
And away it flew
Into the endless sea.

Captain R. Graves, Age 21, of the Royal Welch Fusiliers, Speaks of His War Experience

Every trench had a name, and every intersection of trenches also.

Among the things that every man carried was a handful of biscuits.

Also every man carried one or more wirecutters and hedging-gloves.

Many more men killed themselves or their officers than anyone
let on.

A dead man's face goes white, yellow, gray, red, purple, green, black.

A man is useless for the first three weeks of a war, not knowing
the rules,

And then he is again useless after about nine months, as his nerve
is gone.

It takes about ten years for a man's body to recover from the shock
of war.

Soldiers over forty years old need less sleep but recover poorly from
alarms.

If you go to sleep with wet feet your feet swell remarkably during
the night.

In a heavy rain, trenches fill with quite large numbers of mice,
which drown.

A quite large number of prisoners were killed while being marched
to the rear.

Often bombs would have inside them nails, screws, nuts, bolts, and
clock-parts.

One time when we dissected an unexploded bomb we found a set
of false teeth.

One time after a battle we discovered that every wound incurred
was to the thigh.

One time the trenches flooded so that both sides climbed out to
avoid drowning.

If you removed selected bullets from a machine-gun belt it devel-
oped the rhythm
Of popular songs when it was fired, and sometimes the enemy
responded in kind.
You can smell a dead man for upwards of a mile if the wind is at all
in your quarter.
During one battle our men affixed butcher-knives to broomsticks
with medical plaster.
The number of dead horses and mules on the fields of the Somme
shocked me greatly.
Once I went into a wood filled with the dead and collected their
overcoats for my men.
Once a bird landed among us and spoke in German and the men
came near to killing it.
Officially I was accounted dead in late July and my mother received
a letter to that effect,
However I lived and returned to the front, where soon thereafter I
found a man face down
In the mud. He was the last dead man I saw in France, and like the
first, he was a suicide.

TURK STREET

Once there was a skinny young guy
Named Daniel Pavletich. He lived in
San Francisco and had a sweetheart
Named Nedjelka. She lived on Turk
Street. He lived on Eddy, not far from
Jefferson Square. This was 1941. She
Was eighteen. He was almost twenty.

They both loved messing around with
Radios and car engines and such. Her
Sisters teased her about this and called
Her a grease monkey and greaser girl
But she didn't care and she and Daniel
Bought an old Hudson for ten dollars
From his uncle and worked like crazy
On that thing to make it sing so they
Had a car in which to kiss and cruise,
Which the sisters didn't, *so there!* as
She liked to shout as they drove away.

When the war came and he went she
Made him a tiny radio he could carry
In his pocket which he did from Libya
To Malta to Sardinia to Slovakia where
The Nazis caught him and sent him to
Mauthausen, from which no one returned,

But one day years later a guy shows up
On Turk Street and hands Nedjelka the

Tiny radio and tells her how when Daniel
Heard the Gestapo at the door he knew he
Was done and he tossed his radio to a kid
Who hid it behind the stove until the war
Was over and the kid was almost twenty
And could do what he promised he would.

WHAT IT WAS

We were returning from attacking Fort Drum,
Says my friend Donald, who is really old now,
But then he was a tall skinny kid age nineteen,

And you remember, he says, that we had set out
To blow the fort once before but got sidetracked,
But this time we nailed it hard from every side,

Which was crucial because the fort had firelines
On every way into the bay and we couldn't get
Past it at all, a lot of our guys had died there,

So coming back from blowing it up we were
Feeling good, first because we weren't dead,
And second because we finally shut it down,

So I had my eyes on the water, it was my boat,
You know, and I counted ten bodies in the sea
As we went back to our base. Japanese soldiers,

Yeh, but they were only kids. More than half
I bet only thirteen years old. The Japanese were
Desperate by then and sending their kids to war.

So did we, of course. I wasn't the youngest guy
In the American army, that's for sure. All wars
Are fought by boys sent by old men. That's a fact.

Listen, all these years later I don't regret what I did.
We did the right thing at the time. I'm just telling you
One day I saw dead kids in the water. Yeh, they were

Soldiers, you could say that, but they were thirteen
Years old. That's what I saw. You figure out what
You think about that. I'm just saying what it was.

HANA & DORA

Dora is dark,
Hana is light.

They are sisters
Telling stories.

One day they went to market
And found soldiers in the street.

The soldiers were forcing people
Into long cold silent trains.

Hana saw the soldiers splitting
Families onto different trains so

When a soldier asked *are you sisters?*
She said *who would think such a thing?*

And whirled on Dora who was opening
Her mouth to protest. So it was that they

Stayed together all through the camps,
All through Dachau and Bergen-Belsen.

Remember how we reddened our cheeks
With that bit of crayon, says Dora, so we

Looked healthy so they didn't kill us? Who
would think of such a thing? Only my Hana.

SONG OF THE PARTISANS

Or here's a story. There was a girl named Anna
Born into one war after another. The Bolsheviks
Shot her father and the Nazis shot her husband
And she escaped to London and spent her days
Picking up pieces of bodies for identification and
Burial. At night she wrote songs that no one heard.

One day she hears about Russian partisans battling
The Nazis at Smolensk and something bursts in her
And she writes a song in Russian that smolders and
Burns wherever people hate & fight the Third Reich.
One man comes up to her years later and tells her that
He and four companions were captured by the Nazis

And made to dig their own graves. *To give us spirit*
We whistled your song, he says. She tells him that
She sang the song on the radio twice a day for a year
Until the Nazis finally jammed the signal with static,
But then she learned to whistle the song so piercingly
That they couldn't quell it; nor has anyone else since.

IV

POEMS
IN IRISH

AMHRÁIN ATÁ LEAGTHA
(SONGS & POEMS)

I will tell of Rachturaigh the poet
Whose hand was on the violin also.

It was said that he was *caoch*, a bit
Of sight left in his eye, but this was

Not so: *dall* he was, blind as stone.
But what a tongue in his mouth!

He walked and he wandered,
Hedge to house, saying poems

Which he composed in the night;
And in the morning they sang

In every heart in that house.
That was a miraculous thing.

Ag baint ceoil as stéigeacha cait,
He made music from the guts of cats

Strung on the bit of beech wood
He carried with him everywhere.

If another laid hand to it to play
It would only screech like the cat,

But in the hand of Raftery the blind,
Wonders came from it like waters,

The songs pouring from his throat,
His voice whirling like the winds.

ÁR NATHAIR
(OUR FATHER)

It was my grandfather who taught me the prayer
One sunny morning sitting on front brick steps
As cars and dogs and children went parading by.

Atá ar neamh, who is in heaven, he said, though
Of course He is no He at all in the general sense
But is us and everywhere and that's a stone fact

No matter what your gramma says, don't tell her.
Go naofar d'ainm, hallowed be thy name,
Go dtaga do ríocht, thy kingdom come, which

It is already, as we see by just paying attention.
Go ndéantar do thoil, thy will be done, *ar an
Talamh mar a dhéantar ar neamh*, on earth as

It is in heaven. *Tabhair dúinn inniu*, give to us
Ár n-arán laethúil, our daily bread, and *agus
Maith dúinn ár bhfiacha*, forgive us our debts

Mar a mhaithimidne dár bhféichiúna féin, as we
Forgive our own debtors, which huh we have none.
Well, the prayer as usually promulgated then goes

On to say *agus ná lig sinn i gcathú*, and lead us not
Into temptation, but that's a cruel and foolish line
And I will not teach it to you. So, *ach saor sin ó olc,*

But deliver us from evil, and right there we really
Should say please, but we are Catholics, boy, and no
Polite at all one bit. And then we finish with *amen*,

Which let us say it together as men do, so *amen!*
We said together sitting smiling watching the parade
Which forty years later I do with him still in my heart.

AN CARRAIG (THE ROCK)

One time my gramma was telling stories
Of when she was a girl in the old country
And she hardly ever spoke of her youth so
We boys huddled there silent as she said
In those days we were not to have religion

At all one bit whatsoever, which was hard:
You want to be able to pray with your clan.
So we would wander off from field and fire
At a different hour every Sunday to meet
Under hedge. The soldiers tried to find us

For months. We would choose and mark
The stone on Friday and note the hour
At Saturday market by the number of cows
In Cearan Boland's pen. Finally a soldier
Solved the mystery. He was an Ulsterman.

Well, when the priest lifted up the host,
The man from Ulster shot him in the eye
And priest and bread both fell in the mud.
But years later there came another priest,
This was after the soldiers had gone home,

And this fella finished that Mass, yes he did.
But in the years between those two Masses
There was a thing said, whenever we tired
Of all the battles: *an raibh tú ag an gcarraig?*
Which means, Were you there at the rock?

DINNSEANCHAS
(PLACE-LORE)

I will tell you about my places,
My gramma said to me, and we
Will use the old words for them.

She took out a pencil and paper.
First I will draw the high places.
Here were *cnocáin*, the hillocks,

And over here *leitir*, a rough hill,
And there *seanadh*, the easy hill,
And all of them kneeling before

The *beanna*, the stony mountains.
You see now where I was a girl.
Then she drew all the wet places:

Lathach, a place that was muddy,
And *muing*, the wettest bit of bog,
And *criathrach*, a bog with holes,

And *fiodán*, a stream through a bog,
And then she stopped and I stared
At the map of where she used to be

A deer, a hawk, *a child of the wind*,
Her father called her, in those years
Before they flew across the sea.

QUEEN OF THE WESTERN SEA

Ciúnas ort, quiet on you!
My gramma used to say
To me and my brothers

And wild loud we were,
And heedless and rough,
And there were many weeks

When she was in charge
When mom was bad sick
And dad far away to work

And gramma's voice then
Was the voice of a queen
Like the sea queens in her

Clan line long ago in Clare:
Dún an doras, shut the door!
She'd command, and *ól suas!*

Drink up! And *suigh síos!*
Sit down! Or late at night,
Tucking us in, calling truce,

She would say, quiet and firm,
Bí go maith anois, be good now,
Be at peace, my wild salty boys.

SEANÁTHAIR
(GRANDFATHER)

One time I was with my grandfather
Who was the most dapper man ever
There was in this unbuttoned world,
Such a presence on him, always a tie

And fine shoes and vest and the tiny
Boat of his mustache surfing his lip,
And he started to telling stories one
After another like a string of fish or

Horses or children, each beckoning
To the next to come out of his mouth
And jump into my ears. It was the most
Amazing thing. This went on for hours.

I cannot explain how very rare this was.
That man smiles more than he speaks,
Is how my gramma explained him to us.
How he herded enough words to ask me

For my hand is a wild wonder to me, boys,
And he hasn't said that many words since.
So that one day he started to telling stories
Was a wonder to me altogether absolutely.

One story he told me was about wintering
His nets, how he'd spend weeks and weeks
Silently splicing together strands and then
With a shout cast them into the eager water,

And that story led to a story about a seal,
Which turned out to be really about a lover,
Who turned out to be my gramma, who was
Singing when we came home hand in hand.

BEANNACHTAÍ
(BLESSINGS)

One time I was sitting with my gramma
And I asked her about the Irish and she
Didn't say anything for a moment until
She said: *an béal bocht*, the poor mouth,
Which meant, that language is full of pain.

This I knew already, from the few stories
She told us of her cold ragged childhood,
So I was silent and just hugged her close.
Then she said, *a ghrá*, here are the words
To have, you repeat them after me, love,

And we did, and I remember them all still,
They are bright fish swimming in my mouth:
Grá, which is love, and *aoibhneas*, delight,
And *comhcheol*, which is sweet harmony,
And *beannachtaí*, blessings, a holy word,

And *sonas,* which is happiness, and *lúcháir,*
Which is joy, and *gealgháireach,* or joyous,
And *áilleacht*, which is beauty, and *aontacht*,
Which means unity or wholeness or all things in
Their right places, which was me and my grammy

That evening so very long ago. *A chuisle*, she said,
An rud a théann insa chroí ní scaoiltear as é go brách:
My lovely little boy, what enters the heart never leaves it.

Caoláiteanna
(Thin Places)

Sometimes the old house comes to me in a long dream
And I see it all as it was, children crammed in every room,
The kitchen painted yellow from tip to toe, two small boys
Brawling and bawling in the basement, a long lean teenager
Making sandwiches and a mess, magazines all over, the radio
On always on, the television not, a basketball being bounced
Somewhere it shouldn't be, the mother and the daughter talking
Politics, the phone ringing, the tart old Irish aunt on the other end
Just as the father comes home from work and leans down to kiss
His bride and the new baby boy the roundest happiest kid you ever
Saw, and it's that minute before it's time to start making dinner
When everyone is milling around doing whatever they're doing
And those were grand minutes absolutely and I don't forget them.
They were *caoláiteanna*, places where the holy rubbed up against
The daily, where nothing particularly pressing or important was
Going on, which are of course the most amazing moments of all.

AN FILE AR BUILE
(THE MAD POET)

He was not old, as I thought
A mad poet would be, but
Mad he was for certain since

He did everything backwards.
Slán go fóill! So long for now!
He would say when he met me

In the morning on the road, and
Go raibh samhradh maith agaibh!
Have a good summer! He would say

On the coldest wettest winter day.
This was in our town in America,
Where I was born and to which he

Came as a man. He was short and neat
And always on his way to the library
And me always on my way to school,

Him on his bike and me on mine.
I don't know if he had any English
At all in his head. I had a bit of the Irish

And would say a scrap of it to be polite.
To him maybe it was food for his heart.
One time I was dreaming along and not

Paying attention where I was going and
I crashed into him and we both went down
And he helped me up. It was just after dawn,

As I was on my way to serve the first Mass,
And for once my mind worked at that hour,
And I said *tá an tráthnóna go breá,* which

Means good afternoon to you, and he smiled
And said *gheobhaidh tú an sonas ar phingin,*
Here there are joys as common as pennies.

Is Meiriceánach Mé
(I Am American)

I had occasion after that to see the poet
Here and there as we bicycled past each
Other, and we would exchange greetings
And regards, and one day as he was sitting
On the bench by the library he called out

Boy, how are you? and I said *Tá sé go maith liom*,
It is good with me, and the old words made
Him so happy that I paused a moment to talk.
My gramma had just died and I missed the Irish
In her mouth, and his face had lit so that I sat
And spoke with him there on the golden bench.

I asked him did he write poems really as we all
Thought and he was startled and said o no no,
Is stairaí mé, I am an historian, I collect stories,
And I said *Is maith liom an stair*, I like history,
It's all stories to me, we are learning American
Stories in school and there are so many they are
Like bees around my head all day and all night.

This made him grin and then he said something
I never forgot, because of the way he said it, wry
And sad and pleased and surprised and puzzled
All at once: *Is Éireannach mé*, I am Irish, he said,
And yet *Is Meiriceánach mé*, now I am American.

A moment later we parted, each to find his own
Stories down the years, but the flicker of his face
Stays with me even now, the way he was startled
By the vast ocean between the words in his mouth.

Poems in Irish

CAOINEADH
(LAMENT)

He was a thieving son of a bitch,
God rest his soul.

He never met a man he couldn't cheat,
God grant him peace.

He lied to women and children,
God slake his flames,

And to animals he was a red torment,
God grant him mercy.

He was a man in turmoil from birth,
Said his old father at his wake,

And his life was stone and pain.
Yet we are all thieves and liars at times,

And who among us has not sinned?
And who can measure sin against sin?

Thus, having spoken *caoineadh* over his son,
He sat down and we began to pray.

LINES ON DISCOVERING THE RESULT OF BARRY MCGUIGAN'S CHAMPIONSHIP FIGHT WHILE PAUSING AT A HOTEL IN WICKLOW FOR TEA

O it was a terrible blow,
The face of the proprietress crumpling
As she told me the news,
As if Barry himself had jabbed it,
Which he hadn't
Which was *exactly* the problem
During the bout,
Said her husband the proprietor,
Himself a former boxer
And proud of his past
Although as he said
He hadn't been a whole hell
Of a much of a boxer,
Just a strong little man
Who liked the dodge
And all things considered
Had been good at it,
Like Barry.
I took the county title,
Just that one year,
Wresting it from my own cousin.
O it was a terrible blow
For our mothers the sisters
Their sons hammering away at each other,
Our jabs like the licks of snakes.
Which brings me back to Barry,
Said the proprietress.

He went down in the end,
The tenth it was said her husband
I believe it was the ninth she said
In either case
He fought like a god
And fell down broken
Like Cú Chulainn,
Blood spurting from him
In awful gushets,
Cú Chulainn of the three-colored hair
Cú Chulainn who fought his own brother.
I wish,
Said her husband quietly,
That he would have tied
Himself to the post
Like Cú Chulainn
To the tree where he died.
O it was a terrible blow
Landed by the other fellow
And down went Barry
Blood spurting from him
In awful gushets.

FAOILLEACH
(THE WOLF TIME)

Cú Chulainn had eleven coats, one for every weather:
One from *fia rua*, the red deer of the coldest mountains,
One from *rón glas*, the grey seal of the northern isles,
One from *art dubh*, old bear who is king of the wood,

One from *madra uisce*, the water dog, the river otter,
One from *madra rua*, the red dog, the meadow fox,
One from owl, *cailleach oíche*, king of the night,
One from *cág*, the jackdaw, who struts through the air,

One from *eadar lacha*, the duck people of the north sea,
One from *giorria,* the hares who box each other in spring,
One from *muc mhara*, the porpoise of the sea to the west,
And one from *luch fhéir*, the little mouse in the grass.

Each was given him by the creatures in respect and awe,
As for each he had performed service and sworn fealty
In times of war and strife; for example when *seitheach,*
The wolf, came down on the deer in waves like the sea.

That time Cú Chulainn came to the *fia* when they called,
And routed the wolves so that they never again returned,
But the deer remembered what he said to them that night,
As he prepared to journey back north to his home in Ulster.

The dark will come upon you again, he said, shouldering
His weapons and donning his cloak. It takes many shapes.
That is the way of the world. You cannot evade *faoilleach,*
The wolf times; but you have more weapons than you know.

Having said this he turned to go, with Laeg his charioteer
Attendant upon him, and the creatures of the hills ranked
In silent and respectful rows, when suddenly he said also:
I will be in your heart when you have most need of me.

Those who were there that day remembered his words,
And told them one to another down through the years,
And still those words echo in the hills where the *fía* live,
The mountains in the west which are closest to the stars.

V

PRAYER
POEMS

'Ehyeh-'Asher-'Ehyeh
(I Am Who Am)

of all the things
that have been said
by all the voices
over all the years,
this stays with me
the most of all:
the blunt syntax!

His Holiness The Dalai Lama, Manifestation of Chenrezig, Boddhisatva of Compassion, Stops the Car along the Road to Watch Children Play Soccer

And remembers playing soccer himself long ago,
In Taktser, or Roaring Tiger, in northeast Tibet,
Or what *used* to be Tibet, he thinks darkly, but he is
Too tired to be exhausted, and too used to laughter
To sink into a sometimes-very-welcome despond,
And too interested in the game to miss the moment
Unfolding as a lean lanky girl breaks from the pack

And bears down on the goalkeeper and fakes once
Twice and then lashes a howling shot to the upper
Right corner the goalie leaps and sails and flails and
The shot *just* misses and His Holiness clambers out
Of the car to applaud both the shot and the near-save.
The children turn to see who is clapping but he's no
One they know and no one's dad so they ignore him.

He leans against the warm flank of the car. The driver
Gets out too and lights a cigarette. The game resumes.
Neither man speaks for a moment. The sun is warm.
One day four men came to visit, says His Holiness.
I was asked to choose between two rosaries. I did so.
Then I was asked to choose between pairs of eyeglasses.
I was asked to choose a staff. I did these things. Then

They asked my parents if they might search my body
For the eight holy marks. When they were finished
Examining me they conferred among themselves.
Out behind out house my friends were playing soccer.
They were calling for me to come and play the game.
Lhamo! they called. Lhamo! The men were solemn.
They bowed to my father and my mother, and one man,

The oldest of them, said We have found Avalokitesvara.
Lhamo! my friends were calling. Bring your fast feet!
He is Tenzin Gyatso, the Ocean of Wisdom, said the man.
Also bring your ball because Sonam the idiot lost his ball!
He is Yeshe Norbu, the Wish-Fulfilling Gem, said the man.
Lhamo! If you do not come soon you have to be goalkeeper!
He is Jetsun Ngawang, the Holy Compassionate One,

Said the man, and he made a sign and everyone knelt,
Even my father and mother. For a moment no one spoke,
So I figured they were done with the matter at hand,
And I smiled to think of the game to come, because my
Ball loved the goal, but then the man said, He is Kundun,
The Presence, and everything was different ever after.

HIS HOLINESS THE DALAI LAMA, MANIFESTATION OF CHENREZIG, BODDHISATVA OF COMPASSION, DISCUSSES HIS PREDECESSORS WITH THE DRIVER OF HIS CAR

As they lean against the warm metal flank of it,
The driver smoking a cigarette and His Holiness
Absorbed by children playing soccer in the sun,
The driver asks about this whole reincarnation gig.

Are you really all the reincarnated guys before you?
Well, says His Holiness, my esteemed predecessors
Were incarnations of a wise and holy being, as I am.
Huh, says the driver, pulling long on his cigarette.

Some beings, continues His Holiness, having risen to joy
And understanding, return freely to the ocean of suffering
To be of assistance to other beings. This is who I am,
Or try to be. Which is why I am always on the road

And why I have the honor of your company, Harold.
Who were the other guys before you? asks the driver.
There were thirteen servants before me, says His Holiness.
There was Gedun Drub, who was an austere man, and

There was Gedun Gyatso, who was a poet, and
There was Sonam Gyatso, who loved to travel, and
There was Yonten Gyatso, who swam in strife, and
There was Lozang Gyatso, who had visions, and

There was Tsangyang Gyatso, who wrote love songs.
There was Kelzang Gyatso, who was a scholar, and
There was Jamphel Gyatso, first to meet the West, and
There was Lungtok Gyatso, who died at age eleven, and

There was Tsultrim Gyatso, who died at age twenty, and
There was Khendrup Gyatso, who died at seventeen, and
There was Trinley Gyatso, who died at age eighteen, and
There was Thupten Gyatso, who knew China would eat Tibet.

And now there is only me, always on the road, not dead
Yet. Shall we go? Harold nods and stubs out his cigarette
On the grille of the car. His Holiness bows to the soccer
Players, who do not see him. There are bees everywhere.

YES

I had to choose the clothes the boy would be buried in,
Says the priest, who is not much older than the boy
Was.

I had to decide if he should be buried in the only suit
He owned, or in clothes that he actually wore while
Alive.

I met this boy the night I gave him the last rites.
His name was Johnny and the spirit was in him
Yet.

He was the funniest kid you ever met, said his kid
Sister, and I guess God just then needed some
Laughs.

One time I was with another boy who was about to die,
Says the priest, and I thought he was asleep, but he
Woke

Suddenly and threw his arms around me and begged
Me to tell him there was a god and a heaven. I said
Yes,

I said to him, yes, there is, and you will soon be there,
My child, my poor broken bloody child, yes, yes,
Yes.

LITANY

For the fat girl, prayers.
For the boy with awful zits, prayers.
For the girl weeping on the bench in the rain, prayers.
For those who are moaning, prayers.
For those who keep hoping no matter what, prayers.
For those who just put one foot after the other and walk forward,
    prayers.
For those who haven't the slightest idea, prayers.
For those who say they don't care anymore but they really do,
    prayers.
For the old man who can't remember a thing and knows it, prayers.
For the girl who looks like she's thirteen years old holding her baby
    on the bus, prayers.
For the boy who was raped by his uncle and didn't tell anyone,
    prayers.
For all the fathers who ran away from all their children, prayers.
For all the mothers who didn't, prayers.
For the women who say they don't remember their abortions,
    prayers.
For the children who were sucked out of their mothers, prayers.
For the children who weren't sucked out of their mothers
    and were born into howling hell, prayers.
For those who lie automatically, prayers.
For those who limp, prayers.
For those who lust, prayers.
For those who eat alone at night, prayers.
For those who have sworn to do something
    but hate the thing they have sworn to do, prayers.
For those who shiver, prayers.

For those who retch, prayers.

For those who know the water is bad but they have no choice,
 prayers.

For those who sleep alone at night, prayers.

For those who are afraid of the apartment stairwell at night, prayers.

For those who are only getting into deeper debt and they know it,
 prayers.

For those who cancel the medical insurance
 and hope nothing happens that month, prayers.

For those who can't read, prayers.

For us, far richer than we ever know, prayers.

There Was A Girl Named Sylena

She lived in Staten Island.
She was three years old.
She lived on Boyd Street.
She had three sisters and a brother.
She weighed twenty-two pounds.

Her parents beat her when she soiled her pants.
They scraped her skin with brillo pads.
They poured chemicals on her skin.
To make her stop screaming they made her eat soap.
To make her stop screaming they held her head under water.

We then left her on her side in the water, said her father Matthew.
I checked to see if her chest was rising, said her mother Julie.
I thought we went too far this time, said her mother Julie.
O my God we killed this kid, said her mother Julie.

So here are my questions:
Where is Sylena's ferocious endurance?
Where are her chaotic teenage years?
Where are her four boyfriends and her three sons?
Where is her struggle through community college,
And the day she beaming earned her teacher's degree,
And her unhappy first marriage,
And her peaceful middle years?

And how do we pray enough for her,
Her side pierced with a brillo pad
Her skin anointed with hydrogen peroxide,
Her crucifix an icy tub on Boyd Street?

THE SPLINTERED VOICES OF BOYS PLAYING FOOTBALL IN THE PARK TWO BLOCKS AWAY, IN OCTOBER, HEARD FROM THE FOURTH FLOOR OF AN OLD APARTMENT BUILDING

by a lean young man
just turned twenty-four
just married too and
just back from the war

who sits in the kitchen
near the window
feeding the baby
squash and pea muck and

watching the boys below
and pondering his days
on a moist college field
where he was an end

with huge sure hands
and a violent joy
and muddy humor
that he misses

as he spoons in the muck
and watches a pass spinning
against the wall of cedars
to the open sprinting end

who stretches and *drops it!*
and is razzed by everyone
their cries faint & hilarious
which make the man grin

and rise suddenly to his feet
and hoist his son aloft and
hold him out arms' length
& then pull him in, startled.

In Church
At Lent

An old woman
Has two daughters
Or nieces or
Neighboring girls.

They are not young,
The young women:
Maybe fifty
Each, maybe twins.

The mom reaches
Up to brush back
Their gleaming hoods
As Mass is born.

The two girls stare
At the woman
A tick too long
And I see that

Something is off:
They are too calm.
The girls hold hands
All during Mass,

And look at their
Mother or aunt
Or neighbor lady,
Whomever she is,

For when to kneel,
When to stand, when
To cup their hands
For the sweet bread

In this stark time.
The mother is calm.
Her face is taut,
Her hair stone gray,

Her gestures deft
With her placid
Silent children.
When Mass ends they

Face the mother
Whose patient hand
Flips their bright hoods
Up again. They stand

And holding hands
Still, follow her
Blankly smiling
Into gleaming rain.

GRIEF

For the woman who died today of raging cancer and left two children.
For those two children and their father at the table with her empty
place.
For the way they will only set and wash three dinner dishes
henceforth.
For the way they will stare at her empty place at the table for a long
time.
For the way they will eventually stop staring at her empty place at
the table.
For the way they will eventually unconsciously rearrange themselves
at the table.
For the way they will for a long time cook and eat and talk about
her favorite foods.
For the way they will eventually one day have to try to remember
what those foods were.
For the way they will eventually realize that they have not thought
of her for a whole day.
For the way they will weep when they realize they have not thought
of her for a whole day.
For the way they will weep when they all admit one night they are
furious with her for dying.
For the way they will eventually steel themselves to go through her
clothes and keep only a few.
For the way her favorite gloves will one day surface unexpectedly
from a drawer and cause tears.
For the way the two children will look at each other long and then
silently take a glove each to keep.
For the way they will tell their father about finding her gloves in the
drawer when he comes home,
And for the stagger in his heart when he hears the story and feels
her hands on his face again.

BRUSHING HER HAIR

Well, it's hard,
And we fight every time.
But after a hundred attempts
I've gotten – well, not *good,*
Exactly, but sufficient.
Suffice it to say
That I've learned lessons.
One, be gentle.
Two, go slow.
Three, be quiet.
If I listen she'll talk.
Tonight it was crows and boys.
Wednesday it was noses.
Saturday it was pain.
I could listen to her all day,
But she's in a hurry
To write in her diary
So I finish as slowly
As I can and she runs
Upstairs and I stand there
For a moment, reluctant
To leave this wet chapel.

MAKING OUT

Not in the car,
Not anymore,
Although I could tell you stories.
Not in church,
Except for the kiss of peace,
Which doesn't count.
Here and there hungrily on parting,
And yes here and there on the couch,
And in the hallway suddenly,
And most of all in the kitchen
For reasons that elude me.
Not pressed against the car
Much anymore,
Although here and there, well,
I could tell you stories.
Not in the street,
Although one time,
Some years ago,
Yes on the street,
Desperately,
As if we were both just
Escaped from drowning,
After our infant daughter
Twisted out of my arms in the
Way of spark-muscled babies
And fell for a headlong screaming
Instant until mindlessly my hands
Shot out and juggled and caught her
And lost her again for a second
And then pulled her in for good.
Yes that time, yes,
Our child webbed between us
As we stood there shivering.

VENERATING THE CROSS

At the heart of the Roman Catholic observance of Good Friday is a rite called "venerating the cross," in which a large wooden crucifix is held upright by altar servers so that the congregation may approach and honor it as a symbol of Christ's death and resurrection.

An old man who cannot bend.
His wife who bends.
Her socks are bright blue.
Twin girls, teenagers.
A man who lays his hand
Flat on the crosspiece and weeps.
A priest with cancer,
A teacher whose father died Tuesday.
A woman with a pink hat.
A woman shuffling.
The bare feet, the socks, the slow line.
A girl in overalls.
A girl with loud shoes.
A boy all long bones.
A man from Uganda
A woman with child.
A girl in tears.
A professor of philosophy.
A blind man.
A man who removes his glasses.
A girl who leans forward and rests
Her head against the wood
For an instant.
A very tall man who folds up.
A woman with a large purse.

A man with a cane.
A girl who leaves a lover's kiss.
Another weeping man.
A large man who stays long there.
The choir one by one,
The musicians—oboe last.
A gaping girl led by her mother.
The concelebrants,
One altar boy,
The other,
The end.

PRAYER FOR A FRIEND I HAVEN'T MET

I don't know you
And you don't know me
But I know you are under ether tonight,
And there are knives glinting & your soul is sorely buffeted
To the point where it might flee the scene & in such leaving leave
Irreparable holes in innumerable hearts
Like for no reason every reason mine.

WALKING INTO THE CHAPEL AT THE HOSPITAL

To pray for my son
Who is sedated
After surgery
But doing
As well
As can
Be expected
Says the doctor,
I see a prayer book
Thrown open like a hand
And pause to scribble in it
And above the box where I will scribble
There is this line in a shaky red-ink scrawl:
"Please god wake my boy from his comma"
And I die a little. Later my wife enters the chapel
And finds a man prostrate on the floor in desperate prayer.
That night when we are in bed together her hand is a hawk in
    the dark.

PRAYER IN A FILTHY KITCHEN

Bless us O Lord for these our messes
And lead us not into the overpowering temptation
To nail the kitchen shut with large nails,
To quietly slip the dishes in the garbage,
To lay new linoleum before my wife comes home.
Deliver us from our solemnity
And forgive us the bread crumbs on the floor
The dried pieces of macaroni,
The shatters and crumbles of ginger snaps,
The wrinkled dried peas like tiny brains,
The pen cap long orphaned from its pen,
The splash of pureed sweet potato
That looks like a map of France.
Give us this day our daily task,
Our mop and broom, our drying rack,
The roar of the dishwasher's rattle and clack,
Forever and ever amen.

ALTAR BOY

You button your cassock from the bottom up
To make sure of symmetry before the Lord
And women. When they hand you sweaty coins
To save their husbands' souls, the older women
Grip your fearful wrist for a terrible instant;
Saints are squirming in their heads.

Ignore this vision.
Deposit their moist coins in the box.
Light the wooden taper from a burning candle.
Big candles for Heaven,
Small for Purgatory.
Let them tell you which candle to choose.

An old man said to me once
Big candles for horse-races,
Small ones for the dogs.
He chose the dogs.

When Father motions irritably for the wine,
Ring the bells and bring the wine.
Don't forget to genuflect before the tabernacle.
Wear brown or black shoes.
If Father needs help
With his alb,
Help him.

To Do

I will wake in the morning and listen for the owl.
I will rise and perform my morning ablutions with a light heart.
I will leave the bathroom cleaner than I found it.
I will wake my daughter as gently as possible.
I will make coffee for myself and for my wife.
I will make the children's lunches.
I will cut the crusts off their sandwiches.
I will feed the crow with a broken wing.
I will smell the pregnant air in the pregnant morning.
I will eat a pear and savor every bite.
I will wake my sons as gently as possible.
I will go to work and do my work and come home from work.
I will pay the bills and wash the dishes.
I will fold the laundry and sweep the floor.
I will write letters and plan vacations and cook interesting meals.
I will paint the bedroom and fix the light over the bed.
I will savor the lithe grace and taut honesty of my wife.
I will savor the peculiar humor of my peculiar friends.
I will go to movies and to plays and debate their quality.
I will learn to play an instrument, perhaps the oboe.
I will trim my beard and brush my teeth.
I will listen to my children tell me stories.
I will read stories to them at night in their beds.
I will help them with their homework.
I will look everyone in the eye as I speak.
I will try to remember the color of their eyes.
I will write many books of prose and poetry.
I will wait for epiphanies and revelations.
I will pray quietly and ceaselessly.

I will stare at the mountainous clouds.
I will reel at the reeling of the stars.
I will smile as much as I can.
I will go to the ocean as often as possible.
I will smile all day long if possible.
I will smile in my sleep if at all possible.
I will wake in the morning and listen for the owl.

AT THE THRIFTWAY

One night in the grocery parking lot
I see a woman weeping in her car &
Her engine's running and other cars
Jockey behind her waiting so they
Can get the good spot, you know,
But she doesn't pull out, she just
Sits there with her face streaming

Which I notice as I walk by her car
Because the way she's parked under
The light pole her face is brilliant wet
Though you can't see if she's young
Or old or anything only the gleaming
Tears. I go into the store to get dinner.
When I shuffle out I don't even look

To see if she's still there, such being
The code of our privacy: we weep alone.
But I wonder, while I am driving away,
If maybe someone tapped on her window
And said *Hey lady, here are some prayers,*
Or, more probably, *Hey lady, you leaving*
That spot sometime this week or what?

A Prayer for Gabrielle

She died this morning after the rosary,
The oldest son calling with the news,
And I was desperate to fill the holes
So I told his dad's story how they met.

She was crossing campus one afternoon
As was her habit after the nurses lunched,
And a smiling fellow passing by says Hey,
So they get to talking & he crosses her path

The next few days at exactly the same time,
And things proceed in ways you can imagine
And they end up sharing many years and sons.
I saw her from this window right here, he said,

You never saw a woman with such a dash
In her walk, so I go cross her path, you know,
You get a chance like that maybe just the once,
So here I am, lad, ten times the man I was.

So It Was I Learned to Read

A friend tells me a story about growing up in China.
Her father, a widower, falls ill. Knowing he will die,
He provides for his only child in the ancient fashion:
He sells her into servitude at age ten. She is bought
By a wealthy family with small children, and among
Her many tasks is walking the children to school at

Dawn and waiting patiently by the wall until lessons
Are done. There is a shed in which the servants wait.
My friend, however, chooses to wait by the window,
Through which she can hear the teacher and students.
In this way she learns to read, catching the letters of
The alphabet as they float through the window, and
Writing them in the dirt, and then shepherding them

Into words and then sentences. In the rain it was hard,
She says, but on summer days I learned a lot of words,
As there was good dust in which to write. It is not easy
For me to tell you how it was. The letters had flavors
For me, colors and feelings. Some were cold and dark.
Some didn't want to be words at *all*. The ones at the end
Of the alphabet especially, they were not very friendly.

It took a long time for me to get to know them, she says,
And even today when I write them there is a brief pause
During which we regard each other with care. It is hard
For me to tell you how it was. Some letters just jumped
From the window and others teetered there for a moment
Before they came down to me. So it was I learned to read.

VI

ELEGIES
&
EULOGIES

THE GRAND KAHUNA OF THE ARTS

Poetry is the oldest art
Except for war and sex,

And finding food, and
Propitiating angry gods,

And of course the big one,
The grand kahuna of the arts,

Trying not to get killed. Yes,
That's the king. First you try

Not to get killed and then you
Try like mad to find some food,

Which leads to war and sex
And prayer, which brings us

Right back to poetry, which is
A ferocious war on blindness,

On despair and loss and fear,
And a way to make love wildly,

Eating and praying and singing
About the art of not being killed.

BARRY

In memory of Father Barry Hagan, C.S.C.

No man ever enjoyed a cigarette more than Barry,
And one friend after another in those last weeks
Would wheel him out to the balcony for a smoke,
Even his sister Clare who was always on his case
To quit the nails, as she said. She claimed he first
Pulled smoke at age ten on the porch of the hotel
Where they were raised, by the river in Montana,
Which hotel she said was most definitely *not* a house
Of ill repute despite Barry's many stories to that effect.

Well, in his last few days you had to light the foul thing
For him, he was that weak, and hand it over pronto,
And he'd lean back in his wheelchair and just *eat*
That smoke as if it was the most delicious & necessary air,
The irony of this not lost on him, but he could care less,
As she said smiling, and you had to shake your head
At the man, mere hours left in life but still grinning
And itching to tell that story about when the hotel
Caught fire and out sprinted the old mayor shirtless,
Running toward the bright river fast as he could go.

That Which Has Happened a Billion Times
And Will Happen a Billion Times Again

The way that old men's suit pants bunch up at the knees
When they stand after kneeling in church.

The way some strands of hair work loose
From a woman's ponytail when she is working.

The way some children sleep with one hand open
And legs splayed like scissors.

The way a knee is knobby.
The way a face curves around a grin in middle age.

The way a mouth opens slightly when a man or woman
Falls asleep in a chair by the fire,

And the way they startle gently awake,
Their eyes wide with amazement.

BOLT

Here's a story:
A man tells his wife,
As they are painting a room
For the child they hope to have,
That he has been having an affair,
And his child is due from his lover
In three weeks.

The wife sits down on the floor.
The husband stands there
With his paintbrush.

Or here's another story:
A rivet works loose from a plane
And plummets six miles to earth
Where it strikes a girl in the temple
And kills her.

She's six years old,
Hoeing a field
With her father.

The father sees her crumple
And yells angrily
To quit fooling around.

There's always a story
Like these stories.
No one is strong enough
To carry these stories.

But there they are:
The bolt falling forever,
The husband clearing his throat,
The wife turning
With a half-smile,
Expecting a joke.

THE WIG SHOP

For Doctor Suzanne Tarlov of Nahant, Massachusetts

Would you like human hair?
Asks the shopkeeper,
And I slump in my chair
With a sock on my head
While my friend talks
To the shopkeeper
Who is just trying to be kind.

I was fine until the chemo.
The surgery wasn't so bad,
Considering.

But I find that I am not tough enough
To laugh about things in the wig shop.

I sit and consider the heads of hair.
All different kinds and colors.
There could be so very many of me.

But I leave with the sock on.
A fine sock, ribbed, a deep rich brown,
Very comfortable. Good against drafts.

We drive home.
My friend understands.
I make dinner wearing
The sock, and singing.
My husband understands.
Sock and roll, he says,
His favorite music.

September Eleventh

That was the day the horses refused to leave the barn.
That was the day owls hunched silently in trees.
You could have walked through the forest
Knocking them off branches with a stick.

That day when you opened your mouth to pray
There was only salt. Children bled too easily
And nothing could be done for them.
They wept silently in lobbies and corridors.

That day no one fell in love.
That day the water stank.
That day no one slept
For fear of murder to the east.

You could have walked through the forest
Knocking the owls from the branches,
The owls falling and falling, a shower of owls,
Your mouth sour with smoke, a stick in your hand.

You couldn't close your eyes at all that day,
The children bleeding quietly in hallways,
The owls landing endlessly in the dust, their
Wings useless, your mouth bitter with salt.

SAILBOAT

O
he
said
to her
Set the
stun-sail
and then run
like hell to the
stern but she didn't
know what the stern
was and so ran to port
and the boom just missed
her which caused him to scurry
from the stern to her side and then
for a minute they embraced as if they
were in a terrific storm which to be honest

they were, and I'm happy to report that it lasted forever.

AT SEA

At night Walter shudders without light
Puts his grip on life in glass with his teeth
And hopes his eyes don't roll under the bed
Laughing in the lonely dust, hiding in his shoes.
Walter shivers and pockets his dreams,
Thinks *maybe the whalers will come pick me up*
Folds margarine into bread for tomorrow's
Garden lunch in the grass, sings deafly *O*
white waves and brown girls alive alive o
Marks the day off one more thank god until
Sunday when Mr. Connor with his boat
Comes up the porch to make me alive again
And on the ocean my legs are thickmuscled
Without blue popping veins and
The rough hair is golden and the sun is mine
Walter dips his bread in grease for dinner
white and brittle like an eggshell now
but i slept on oily wood, morning steamy
with the carcasses of monsters o i lived
Walter huddles under his sheet and rocks
Seeing the greentops of mountains at the foot
Of the bed, off starboard; and forgetting the dark
He squints a tan and a smile
And watches the sun without blinking . . .
here we go boyos the islands of steamy green

LACRIMAE RERUM
(Tears for Things)

My quiet uncle's linen waistcoat, buried with him many years ago,
And now with him under elm on a hill high above the city he loved.

My quieter other uncle's sigh as he put down his beer can by his
chair,
And the sinewy leather of his hands and the sweep and leap of
his hair.

The way I used to be so sure that my wife was the only woman
for me,
And that I was the only man for her, and that nothing could ever
part us.

The way I would hoist my daughter's tiny legs in the air with my
left hand
And powder her with my right hand and tickle her and lean down
to touch

My capacious nose against her tiny nose and be lost in the sea of
her stare.
Now she is a tall ship heading ever further to sea, and I am happy
for her,

And proud, and hip to her independence, and mature about all
these changes,
But I remember, I remember, and sometimes there are sudden tears
for things.

TIDE

One time,
When we were
All eating dinner,
The whole clan
Twenty strong
Around the table,
Dad at the head
And the youngest
On a lap somewhere,
The little kids watchful
And silent & grinning,
The stories got longer
And louder and my sister
Got up to get more wine
As all three of my brothers
Laughing shouting corrected
Each other and I saw my dad
Trying to get his oar in the water,
But he couldn't break in and
There was no pause for him
When he cleared his throat
When he said *Well I'll tell...*
And no one noticed him
And I didn't say anything,
And he leaned back in his chair
And he fell to listening
And things were different
Ever after.

Rules for Vessels Navigating
the Harbors, Rivers, and Inland Waters
of Love, Including Gulfs & Streams
Experiencing Reduced Flow

(thanks to the Pacific Coast Pilots' Guide, 1926 edition)

In thick weather, when approaching danger,
Soundings should be taken continuously.
Compasses become in time slightly in error,
And magnetic force diminishes with distance.

When vessels are running in the same direction,
And the vessel which is astern should desire to pass,
She shall give one short blast of the whistle,
As a signal of such desire,
And if the vessel ahead answers with two blasts,
Shall put her helm to starboard.

Or if the vessel ahead does not think it safe
For the vessel astern to attempt to pass at that point,
He shall immediately signify the same by giving
Several short and rapid blasts of the whistle,
Not less than four.

The vessel ahead shall *in no case* attempt to cross the bow
Or crowd upon the course of the passing vessel.

Conditions at their worst produce broken water and heavy,
    choppy seas
From all directions, which make it difficult to keep control.
Counter-currents and eddies may occur near straits,
Rips and swirls occur over shoals and uneven bottoms.

Every vessel shall, in fog, mist, or storm, go at moderate speed,
Having careful regard to the existing circumstances and conditions.

A vessel hearing the fog signal of another vessel,
The position of which is not clearly ascertained,
Shall, so far as the circumstances of the case admit,
Stop engines and then navigate with caution
Until danger of collision is over.

A vessel which is running free shall keep out of the way
Of a vessel which is close-hauled.

A vessel with the wind up
Shall keep out of the way of the other vessel.

As regards buoys and other fixed points of navigation,
Too much reliance should not be placed
On their always maintaining their fixed position.
It is safer to navigate by continual soundings.

As regards lights, the glare of a powerful light is often seen
Far beyond the limit of visibility of the actual rays of the light,
But this must not be confounded with the true range.
Similarly a weak light is easily obscured by haze.

In employing the horizontal danger angle,
Charts from previous sources should *not* be used.

In cases of shipwreck, remain by the wreck until assistance arrives.
Remember that on your coolness will greatly depend your chances
    of success.

Vessels underway successfully shall display
A clear, uniform, and unbroken light.

COPSE

After
My mother
And father
Leave to fly home
I sweep every room in the house
And mop the kitchen floor until it squeaks
And cut my fingernails and trim my beard
And cut the children's fingernails and fold
The laundry and start a new load and clean
Out the lint trap and pick up the playroom
And put away the newspapers and books
And so debate and distract the rising sadness:

But it floods and so I make tea
And sandwiches for the children, and
In the choosing of breads and trimming of crusts,
In the blading of jam and slabbing of butter,
The hiding of two ginger snaps under two squares of sandwich each,
There is little grove of trees in which I stand for a moment quietly.

MISS MARY MARGARET

Well, she died on a Saturday, late in the evening,
And was buried Wednesday afternoon in the rain.
Her coffin was made of poplar, which she would
Have savored, as poplars always reminded her

Of cypresses and Italy. One time, she told me, she
Really did sing for her supper, in a café in Puglia,
Having mislaid her purse, and whereas this was a
Woman who had sung at the Metropolitan Opera,

The patrons, initially startled and skeptical, stood
In respect when she was finished. I sang Puccini
Of course, she said. O the songs I sang in theaters
And churches and chapels and auditoria and halls,

O the way my legs shook the first time I sang
In public, I was all of fourteen. I sang Puccini
Of course. O the thousands of music students I had
Later in life, the off-key boys and the diva girls,

The glower of mothers and patter of fathers,
You would think the saving grace would be
The great students, the talents, the extraordinary,
But no, it is the ones without talent who worked

As hard as they could whose faces are still with me,
Their tongues between their teeth, their eyes haunted.
And o the men I loved who did not love me,
And the men who loved me whom I could not love!

Yet I did have children, my three burly sweet nephews,
O I ferried them to music lessons in my old Plymouth
And then to my house for burgers and bottles of beer,
O the walks we had on the beach and the bicycle rides,

And the shucking and sucking of oysters and the trips
With their auntie to the great cities of the east, which
Aged me by a thousand years. But I know when I die,
When they are men, they will carry me from the church

On their endless shoulders and they will weep and sing
And then they will go to my house for burgers and beer,
And one among them, the oldest, will search all night
For my pitch-pipe, which he will keep the rest of his days.

POEM FOR HENRI NOUWEN

The way he leaped up suddenly from the table
To make a point with the whole wild exclamation
Point of his body and the way his arms swirled
And swung and whirled and danced cheerfully
Around his cheerful face as he spoke and the way
As soon as he sat down he leapt up again to agree
Utterly and wholly from the bone of his being
With what you said rather than find the certain
Hole in what you said but then leaping off from
What you said he would say something so new &
True and clear and refreshing and you wished you
Carried a notebook just for Henri but pausing to
Keep track of the swoop and zest of his thought
Would ruin the whole joy and verve of the thing
Which was a thing never before in the world and
Never again which was the sort of thing that gave
Henri a bubbling childish brilliant genius holy joy
Which was pretty much the point of Henri,
And what we miss most.

MEN: OPERATING INSTRUCTIONS

Open carefully; contents under pressure.

Caution: sharp edges. Contents may cause injury.

Contents may have shifted during transportation.

Caution: nuts may have come in contact with contents.

Contents packed by volume; individual units may differ in weight.

Caution: the surgeon general has determined that contents may
be mule-

Headed, doltish, rude, stubborn, defiant, forgetful, easily distracted,
liable

To repetitive pattern for sheer simplicity's sake in this vale of fears
and tears,

Difficult to penetrate or understand, complicated beyond imagina-
tion, and not

At all what you thought you wanted when you were a kid dreaming
of princes.

Open with care. The manufacturer recommends mercy & humor.
Do not microwave.

Credits

Many of these poems first appeared in magazines, and I thank the discerning editors of those periodicals for their encouragement and for not howling with laughter when they opened my envelopes stuffed with things that demanded a good stretch of the imagination to be called poems in any orthodox sense of that ancient and august word. So:

"Lines On Discovering The Result of Barry McGuigan's Championship Fight While Pausing at a Hotel in Wicklow for Tea" appeared in *The American Scholar*, published by the Phi Beta Kappa Society in Washington, D.C. Thanks to Robert Farnsworth and to the very fine essayist Anne Fadiman.

"Altar Boy," "Jupiter," "What to Pack" and "At Sea" appeared in *First Things*, published by the Institute on Religion and Public Life in New York.

"Joe in the Dark" and "Holding a Swift," appeared in *The Christian Century*, published by the Christian Century Foundation in Chicago. Thanks to poetry editor Jill Pelaez Baumgaertner.

"Prayer in a Filthy Kitchen" appeared in *Fireweed: Poetry of Western Oregon,* published in Eugene, Oregon. Thanks to editor Ann Staley.

"Henri" appeared in *Remembering Henri: The Life and Legacy of Henri Nouwen*, published by Orbis Books. Thanks to editors Fr. Gerry Twomey and Fr. Claudio Pomerleau.

"Walking Into the Chapel at the Hospital" appeared in *Yankee Magazine*, published in Dublin, New Hampshire; thanks to managing editor Tim Clark, now a high school teacher, a brave and admirable change of career, Timotheus.

"Prayer for a Friend I Haven't Met" and "Death of a Phoebe" appeared in the *Alaska Quarterly Review*, published by the University of Alaska at Anchorage.

"Sailboat" and "Brushing Her Hair" appeared in *U.S. Catholic*, published by the Claretians in Chicago; thanks to Tom McGrath and Maureen Abood.

"Her Side" appeared in *Oregon Quarterly* from the University of Oregon, an excellent magazine; thanks to editor Guy Maynard.

"That Which Has Happened A Billion Times And Will Happen A Billion Times Again" appeared in *Wabash College Magazine*; thanks to editor Steve Charles.

"The Honorable Edmund Burke Addresses My Twin Sons as They Sulk in Their Room After a Terrific Fistfight" and "The Flogging of Charles Maher, Norfolk Island, 1823," appeared in *The Recorder*, the journal of the American Irish Historical Society; thanks to editor Christopher Cahill.

"To Do" appeared in slightly goofier form in *The Central Catholic High School Quarterly*, published by said high school in Portland, Oregon, and traded to smiling then-editor Casey Peddicord for a Central Catholic High men's basketball practice jersey. Who says poets never get paid?

The two Dalai Lama poems appeared together (fittingly) in the webzine *Nimble Spirit* (www.NimbleSpirit.com), the brainchild of the fine writer and editor Michael Wilt.

"Nine" appeared in *The National Catholic Reporter,* courtesy of the courteous editor Patty McCarty.

"Instructions to the New Puppy" and "Turk Street" appeared in the excellent webzine *Smokebox* (www.smokebox.net). Thanks to peculiar editors Marc Covert and John Richen.

"Abhrain ata Leaghta" appeared in *Fugue,* a journal made at the University of Idaho, and my thanks to editor Jeff Jones, who paid for it in good red wine. See, poets *totally* get paid.

"Ar nAthair (Our Father)" appeared in *OnLineCatholics,* a terrific webzine in Australia (onlinecatholics.com.au). My thanks to the deft bright editor Kate Mannix.

My thanks especially to the fine Limerick and Oregon poet Ger Killeen for his help with my rough raw Gaelic (and if you have not read Ger's three books *A Wren, A Stone That Will Leap Over the Waves,* and *A Trace of Exaggeration,* you should, really) and to Seamas O Neachtain, whose column on Irish in *The National Hibernian Digest* often prompted my poetical misadventures.

"Lilies" appeared in the gentle magazine *Writing Nature*, edited by the gentlemanly J. Parker Huber in Brattleboro, Vermont.

"Goose Arrested at the Corner of Summer & Winter" appeared in *Orion*; my thanks to energetic young editor Tara Rae Gunter.

"Grief" appeared in *America*; thanks to the terrific poet Paul Mariani.

"At the Thriftway" appeared in the journal *Literature and Belief.* Thanks to the deft poet Lance Larsen and his essayist colleague Patrick Madden of Brigham Young University.

"September Eleventh" appeared in *The Oregonian* newspaper in Portland. Thanks to generous editor Peggy McMullen.

"Captain Graves, Age 21, of the Royal Welch Fusiliers, Speaks of His War Experience," is, as you might well suspect, drawn unadorned from the novelist and poet Robert Graves' haunting memoir *Good-bye to All That*, originally published in 1929. Prayers on Graves' soul in the lee of the Light.

Credits

143